MW00915615

1000 REASONS TO STAY SINGLE:

An Independent Person's Companion
Picture Book

IN ASSOCIATION WITH BELLE BAX BOOKS

Affirmation, Manifestation, Dream Journals,

Humor Journals, and Blank Journals

INDEPENDENTLY PUBLISHED

BY BELLE BAX

1000 REASONS TO STAY SINGLE:

An Independent Person's Companion Picture Book

MASTER THE MINDSET OF COMPLETING YOURSELF

1000 Reasons to Stay Single: An Independent Person's Companion Picture Book by Belle Bax

Published by Belle Bax

Cover by Belle Bax

ISBN: Hardcover ISBN: 9798823952521
ISBN: Softcover ISBN: 9798823950831

Published in the United States

First Edition

For the wild and free among us.

Table of Contents

INTRODUCTION

Single-dom can be a harsh experience, whether or not you're happy alone. What to say to the family, friends, and nosy neighbors? Society sells partnership as the end-all be-all. (When will they learn?)

Sometimes, it is a rather lonely and daunting experience, especially when events roll around like weddings and dinners. No one likes to be the third wheel, so sometimes there's no choice but to sit out. So, why are you single? Perhaps there are no viable options. Or maybe you just enjoy your own company!

It could be that you feel a bit heart broken and need time to heal. No one seems to understand.

Well, Cinderella, or Prince Charming, here are exactly one thousand reasons why it's actually better to stay single, for now. One Thousand Reasons to Stay Single: *An Independent Person's Companion Picture Book* is your official partner in crime.

HOW TO USE THIS COMPANION BOOK:

Read each reason in order, or close your eyes, turn to any page and choose with your pointy finger for a wonderfully serendipitous boost.

Feeling creative or bored? Color in the images. Don't worry about staying inside the lines!

What happens in Single-dom, stays in Single-dom.

Cheers!

CHAPTER 1

Single-dom With Benefits

Are you single for life or is this just a little break? Do you have some internal work to do on yourself or do you just prefer your own company? Are you heartbroken and swear you'll never love again? Are you taking the time to look inwards and exercising your autonomy to find what strength lies inside? Are you forced to be alone at the moment and need an upside? Sometimes we just need a little time to work out the rough patches until we're ready for that "perfect someone". Some of us are mad geniuses who happily resonate with the single life in ways that might seem odd to, well, pretty much everyone. Some of us simply want to shout, "I'm free and happy! Leave me alone!" Well, whatever your reason, the good thing is, if you see it below, you know you've got company. If you don't see it below, then our list is simply growing. In the end, there are plenty of fish in the sea who feel just as you do! There are fantastic reasons to stay single and amazing benefits to extended alone time. Some of them are:

1. I get to enjoy my own company, something I very much prefer.

2. I don't have to force my life to fit the mold of another. I'm content with my life.

3. I get to enjoy sex the way I prefer it: without strings – it's more my thing.

4. I have more confidence in myself knowing that I am happy alone.

5. I am waiting for Mr. or Mrs. Right and I'm honestly fine on my own 'till then.

6. I am free to not share my body at all.

7. Less drama.

8. Mostly I just don't feel like talking!

9. Time is fluid and so am I.

10. Weekends with no plans means more time to concentrate on my wants and desires (and I desire a whole day in bed.)

11. I am healing from the past and need time alone.

12. I am checking off my bucket list (see Chapter 2).

13. It's harder to be wrong when you're alone.

14. I am a deep thinker and can't do people.

15. I like to transmute my love for one to unconditional love for all, and it comes back to me ten-fold. I never feel alone!

16. I am too feisty to be tied down.

17. Dating is too exhausting for me.

18. More people are staying single for life. I'm part of a growing movement.

19. I'm a clairsentient empath and other people's constant energy overwhelms me. I would need to live in a house with a separate wing and I haven't found anyone who would agree to that yet (plus I can't afford that big a place).

20. I can love whomever I'm with without needing to worry about how the relationship is defined.

21. There's one less set of crazy parents to deal with.

22. The closet is organized the way I like it.

23. I'm a little too confused at the moment to focus on, wait, what was I talking about?

24. I don't have to pay for everything all the time.

25. Cooking naked with a pep in my step.

26. Being in a relationship is mentally expensive and I'm broke.

27. I don't want to be "we".

28. I have trouble telling the truth.

29. I can get better at understanding love when it is self generated.

30. I believe in divine encounters and hate dating apps, so if they don't show up, it wasn't meant to be. I'm in tune with the universe.

31. I don't want to have to worry about divorce.

32. It's quiet – I'm single and find it to be the most peaceful time in my life.

33. The toilet seat can stay up!

34. The toilet seat stays closed!

35. I want to spend all my time reading scripture.

36. I'm working on my third PhD.

37. I'm robosexual.

38. I'm afraid of the unknown.

39. I'm a badass with internet fame and no time for just one.

40. I have big trouble understanding social cues and am still trying to figure out how to navigate my wonderful uniqueness before I can entertain another.

41. I can't stand to watch people chew their food.

42. I don't want someone around me all the time.

43. I have the freedom to travel (there's so much to see!).

44. Now that I'm single, I know myself better than I ever have.

45. No passive-aggressive comments.

46. I like to live unpredictably.

47. I can flirt without there being an issue.

48. I am a nun.

49. I am a priest.

50. I am a monk.

51. I am a healer on a mission and I belong to everyone.

52. I have time to work on my inner world and my feelings of not being good enough.

53. I can't stand the cattiness that I have to endure when I'm in relationships.

54. Stinky bathroom, no problem.

55. I'm overflowing with ideas and there isn't enough time in the day to accomplish it all, let alone share it with someone else. (Chapter 2!)

56. I practice non-attachment – All is temporary.

57. No one to let down.

58. I like to take it day-by-day, and it's daylight savings time.

59. I am hibernating and will soon become a butterfly.

60. I am still letting go of toxic situations and people.

61. I am transhuman and 1101100 1101111 1110110 1100101 100000 1101001 1110011 100000 1101000 1101001 1100111 1101000 1101100 1111001 100000 1101001 1101100 1101100 1101111 1100111 1101001 1100011 1100001 1101100.

62. I'm an old soul: my mission here is to sit under a metaphorical tree, like Siddhartha.

63. I have married myself and have the certificate to prove it.

64. I haven't met "the one".

65. "The one" got away.

66. I am trying to find my Dharma.

67. Finding someone won't "fix" me.

68. I am finishing my degree.

69. I've been searching for an angel in white and I can feel them but they're nowhere in sight.

70. I have kids and can't get a minute to myself, and I'm kind of good with that.

71. I won't end up on the couch after an argument.

72. People just disappoint me.

73. I am too busy pushing the boundaries of what is possible for myself, and first on the list is item one. Soon. Very soon.

74. I'm in love with two people and can't figure out whom to choose.

75. I'm only here for the snacks, then I have to return to the future.

76. I am struggling with accessing my feelings and I'm afraid I have none.

77. I can choose whatever pet (or pets) I like.

78. I have the space to establish all the good habits I wish to master. These can be carried into a future relationship, if I choose to go that route.

79. I am a player. (Actually, I'm afraid I will get hurt one day, so I need the freedom until I can get to the bottom of my fears.)

80. I can keep doing my favorite gross habits.

81. I'm afraid to show my belly and cellulite to a new person.

82. I need to focus on my health and wellbeing before I have room in my life for another.

83. I can have whole, entire, conversations with myself out loud. I am very funny and make excellent conversation.

84. I'm a sleepwalker who generally scares the living daylights out of people in the middle of the night.

85. I'm a shaman who must search for eternity about the eternity.

86. I am letting go of all my earthly possessions to squeeze only what I can get into one backpack and that's all I know so far.

87. I can barely take care of myself.

88. I'm battling severe depression and need to seek out a way to get help, either through trusted friends or by searching for an organization near me, because the truth is, I am worth it.

89. I'm worried they'll think I'm not as attractive once I take my makeup off.

90. I'm working undercover as a "Remote Viewer" for a secret government program and can't be coupled. (Also, I'm watching you now.)

91. I want to travel the world first.

92. I want to dedicate all my time to my future.

93. I don't have to worry about being faithful – I find this stressful.

94. I just want to party.

95. I can eat an entire pizza and then stare at the ceiling with unabashed comfort food stomach.

96. I am too busy training to walk through walls by acquiring sufficient hyperspace energy. Yes, it's a thing. Patented.

97. I am emotionally unavailable so might as well save everyone the time!

98. I'm camping solo right now.

99. I live in an underwater science dome and am very satisfied with all my alone time.

100. I'm on a mission to terraform the world's deserts and bring water to thirsty nations.

101. I'm still trying to heal childhood wounds.

102. I generate the best work when I am alone and that's all I care about right now.

103. I can sleep in as late as I want without judgment.

104. I find most interactions with people superficial, partner or not.

105. I can get affection without commitment.

106. I have Objectophilia.

107. I always hurt the ones I love.

108. I'm still working on my language of love.

109. I'm an eccentric genius.

110. I see dead people. I have to deal with that first.

111. Relationships are too much work.

112. I'm a rocket man.

113. I'm a rocket woman.

114. I'm a rocket person.

115. "They" are after me and I'm on the run.

116. This is all a simulation so what's the point?

117. I am at one with divine consciousness; there is no beginning and there is no end, we are all one, so I am never alone.

118. I need to concentrate on my work.

119. I still live with my mom.

120. I am presently unhappy and I don't want to bring my unhappiness into a relationship.

121. I am breaking generational curses.

122. I am too easily distractible and have huge goals – so can't do serious right now.

123. No one to distract me from my spiritual connection to the Divine.

124. I work so much. I can't seem to find the time to even think about meeting anyone.

125. No one to judge my religious beliefs.

126. I'm in the middle of a startup.

127. I have been living my whole life through people and I want to give it a go on my own for a while.

128. Relationships are not the end goal.

129. Settling down makes me feel old.

130. I have too much on the line.

131. I brainstorm better when I'm alone.

132. I struggle with same sex attraction but am not ready to fully engage with this part of myself.

133. I am preparing for the Olympics.

134. No loud snoring sounds when I'm trying to sleep.

135. I can harness my unused sexual energy in other ways like working out, creative pursuits, or manifestation

136. Cake at midnight!

137. I am a Starseed waiting for my ship to come get me. (Once I finish my mission, that is.)

138. There are many fish in the sea and I get to fish whenever I want for however long I want.

139. I don't feel lonely when I am alone.

140. I can't stand small talk.

141. I'm afraid I'm going to be like my parents.

142. I can burn all the candles and incense I want.

143. Other people's emotional baggage burdens me.

144. People can't keep up with me.

145. I've already been married and I'm just done.

146. I'm still working on the Collatz Conjecture, will get back to you in just a...

147. I don't like to be touched.

148. I lower my expectations by choosing no-one and am happy that way!

149. I have to manifest everything on my vision board before I feel ready to join forces with someone else.

150. I meet my own needs.

151. I don't believe in true love.

152. I believe in true love but I can't do dating apps. Does anyone approach in person these days?

153. I have goals that I have to meet before I feel good enough.

154. I am a "low energy" person and prefer to be alone.

155. I don't want to lose myself in a partnership.

156. I can stay up as late as I want without disturbing anyone.

157. My life is less predictable. There's newness everywhere I go.

158. The things I want to do don't require a partner.

159. I am emotionally independent and want to keep it that way.

160. I'm working on trust after terrible deceit.

161. Smaller house means less rent and I'm a penny pincher.

162. Every day the world get's stranger and stranger and now I'm not even so sure I'm completely human.

163. I want to adopt and be a single parent.

164. I am battling addictions, so for now, my priorities are me.

165. I don't like having to be responsible for appearances (especially happy couple social media shots).

166. I like all the attention I get from being available.

167. Entertaining other people's friends and family is extremely draining for me.

168. I'm turning my side-hustle into a full blown career and need every waking moment to see it to fruition.

169. I have to wait until my parents approve of my sexuality or I will lose my inheritance.

170. I don't have to worry about anyone eating the thing I was going to have later.

171. I don't have to pretend "it" was good.

172. I'm bad to the bone.

173. I am working on being more generous.

174. Being "on" all the time for someone else is tiring.

175. I can go to the movies alone and not worry about finding two seats.

176. I'm too nice and will most definitely get taken for granted.

177. I am good enough by myself.

178. I have just lost so much and I am still grieving.

179. I feel like I make a lot of dumb mistakes. I have all the space I need to work on trusting myself.

180. I like the chase.

181. I have a hard time being myself with others.

182. I'm an activist and only care about my cause.

183. I can try new things and stop them without being accused of dabbling.

184. An empty house is a freedom playground.

185. I am hyper-focused on completing a thesis.

186. I need less stimulation than most people.

187. People in relationships seem too dependent.

188. I'm truly confused about what it is that I'm supposed to look for in a partner.

189. No more getting iced out.

190. Every day can be self-care day.

191. The lights are how I like them.

192. I'm all I can handle.

193. I don't want to change my habits or routine.

194. I don't want babies.

195. I have to figure out my purpose before I can take on someone else's.

196. I've figured out my life's purpose but I am still working on how to get there.

197. I am waiting for important news before I can decide my next step.

198. I'm healing from some things I'm still unclear about and have no idea where to start.

199. I don't want to end up in a mediocre relationship because I feel there's something wrong with being single.

200. I value my own advice and ask myself for it often.

201. The temperature is just how I like it.

202. I can season my food extra spicy, just like me.

203. I can figure out what my work life balance is.

204. I feel like I'm supposed to be with someone I'm divinely guided to be with but they have run away. (It's a special Twin Flame Journey that's hard for others to understand.)

205. I want to be a single and sexy Fireman.

206. I can't find anyone that likes the same things that I do.

207. I believe I'll meet the right person when I'm supposed to. I'm not going to force it.

208. I'm demisexual and no one's vibes are a divine match for me, yet.

209. I don't want negotiations and compromises over this and that.

210. I don't have to do anyone's laundry, get stuck with the dishes, pick up messes, pay for everything or feel generally taken for granted.

211. I don't have to change anyone's oil, take out the garbage, fix the disposal, pay for everything or feel generally taken for granted.

212. My nerves are too frayed for a relationship and time alone helps me heal.

213. I got a tarot reading that said I have bad karma to pay for from a past life with my next mate.

214. I'm not accidentally married to an energy vampire.

215. My contact lenses are not confused with their contact lenses.

216. I can be alone when I get sick.

217. My friends are enough.

218. My life just got hit with a storm and I don't want anyone to be subject to it's chaos.

219. I have too much stuff and there is no room for a person in my space.

220. I'm not into romance.

221. I feel lost in space.

222. I don't have to tiptoe to the fridge for a midnight snack.

223. I'm just really angry and jealous all the time and know I need to work through all these feelings.

224. I come from a strict background and can't find anyone within my group so I get to date secretly. It's fun!

225. I am on a mission that requires me to live and travel alone. I don't want to fall in love and then have to choose between passions.

226. I don't want to lose my sense of determination.

227. Walking a path alone fulfills me.

228. There is an entire universe to discover, including 13 billion years of history.

229. I place my things where I want them.

230. I have to deal with my anger issues before I can have a healthy relationship.

231. I am waiting until I feel I look better in my jeans, then, watch out world!

232. All my friends married for money and status, and I'm just sickened by it all.

233. I am secretly in love with someone I can never have so why hurt another person? I'd be faking it. I get to stand in my authenticity, which is paramount.

234. No wondering how they really feel.

235. I am becoming a better observer every day.

236. I am too irrational to be in a relationship.

237. I am not kind to myself so there is no way I can be kind to another.

238. I can throw a singles party and make my partnered friends feel left out (and then

throw one for them later because I love them too).

239. I can sing out loud, really loud, if I want to without an audience.

240. No one is rolling their eyes at me when I'm "not looking".

241. I rear the kids with my rules!

242. I can be sure I'll never turn into my parents.

243. I filleth my own cup and I'm liking what it's filled with.

244. I feel as if relationships attract too much conflict.

245. It is not in the cards for me to settle down.

246. I'm a loner.

247. I have released the fear of being alone.

248. I am a gorgeous flirt and I cannot be tied down.

249. I find the entire world of partnership odd, animal kingdom-ish and antiquated.

250. I won't catch colds from my signifiant other.

251. My hormonal issues are my own to deal with.

252. I am a traveling star of the stage.

253. When I meet someone, I am more open to experiencing them rather than capturing them.

254. I can feel my match is near but they haven't shown up yet.

255. Being alone is a luxury that some people can only dream about.

256. I'm into myself more than other people and that's all there is to it.

257. How much money I need is up to me.

258. I can sit in the dark and listen to the silence.

259. It's easier to isolate my preconceived notions. For example: it's possible to be in a relationship and still be lonely so I challenge my reactions to emptiness with self-love.

260. I don't have to concern myself with how I look, or smell.

261. Beard, mustache, armpit or leg hair, eyebrow shape, facial fuzz, facial and body jewelry, tattoos, and hair styles are my own decision and aren't up for debate (or subtle side-eye.)

262. I am on a solitary mission to visit the most unexplored and mysterious places on Earth.

263. I can sleep in whatever bizarre-in-appearance, yet strikingly comfortable, position I want.

264. I'm still discovering how I present and want to do it without debate or judgement, however well-meaning.

265. I tend to sabotage anything that begins to work in my favor.

266. Relationships make me feel tense and on edge.

267. Everyone is still asleep on this pesky spaceship. Oh well, I'm kind of digging this A.I.

268. I travel for work and am never in one city long enough to commit to anyone. I love my job!

269. I am separated by a long distance from the one I truly love. We have plans to get serious in the future. In the meantime, I really enjoy my autonomy.

270. I want to join the circus.

271. I can fall asleep wherever I want without judgment.

272. No one to judge my masterpiece when it's halfway finished.

273. I'm taking care of a relative and unfortunately there is no pragmatic way to have a relationship right now.

274. I don't have to worry about being cheated on.

275. I look, feel and act much younger than my age which leaves me fewer options, so I choose to fly solo.

276. I don't have to hide the mail.

277. I am rebelling against tradition, just because.

278. I am more interested in solving the injustices of the world than being in a relationship.

279. I have all the space I need to shift my relationship with money, lack and abundance.

280. I can remodel the house the way I like it and make the whole thing my he/she shed.

281. Life is more adventurous when I'm free and alone.

282. I feel numb.

283. I still feel like a child.

284. I don't know how to tell if the love I feel is real.

285. Less next-day brain fog from late night dates.

286. No one has control over outcomes and being in a relationship only heightens a sense of false security.

287. I have a great excuse to experiment in the kitchen.

288. I have deep blockages that I can't understand and am absolutely loving the time alone to get to know myself.

289. I'm too rich to trust anyone.

290. I am working two jobs to get on my feet.

291. I would rather tinker with my inventions all day than focus on someone else.

292. I can pass gas without an audience and don't have to worry about smelling anyone else's.

293. I've been hurt in the past.

294. I have twelve cats, a horse, two chickens, a dog, and a duck. There is not a moment or spare space for another being in my life.

295. I save money on gifts.

296. I save money on food.

297. I'd rather write about relationships than be in one.

298. Forgetting to brush my teeth ain't great but it's my problem.

299. I'm just not interested in relationships at this time. I have no reason.

300. I will never get over my ex.

301. Less chance I realize I married a psychopath or abuser by accident.

302. No arguments over whether the dog can or can't sleep in the bed.

303. Eating out of the jar.

304. I'm a rockstar.

305. I decorate how I want to decorate.

306. I seem to be remembering my dreams more easily without another person in my space. The one's I have at night, and the goals I had as a child. It's exciting.

307. The dirty laundry can pile up and I can clean on my own schedule.

308. My heart is broken. I can give myself all the space I need to heal.

309. I can look into things, like UFO's or Big Foot, without it being "a thing".

310. I can spread out on the bed.

311. I am leading a powerful company and I really have no time for a relationship, though one day I might be open to it.

312. I don't have to sneak new purchases into the house.

313. I don't have to listen to uninteresting stories.

314. My email is MY email.

315. I don't feel trapped.

316. I am a big commercial director and never in the same city for long.

317. Less mind games.

318. Rejection is something I am not willing to experience.

319. I can wear my comfy undies.

320. I'm still married but separated.

321. I make my own rules!

322. I'm a pop star who signed a contract to appear like I'm single.

323. I feel the most at ease with myself.

324. Honestly, I'm kind of afraid of people.

325. If I make a mistake while cooking I'm not responsible for anyone else's low blood sugar.

326. I can scroll through social media without it being a thing.

327. My debt is my only debt.

328. I have kids and that's enough for me.

329. I like dinner's to be party of one.

330. My life is more mysterious.

331. I am working through childhood wounding.

332. I can choose whatever type of mattress works for me.

333. Pressure is off – I am the Joneses and I only need to keep up with myself!

334. No one to ruin my day.

335. It can be really fun to be selfish.

336. I can decompress in my own way after a busy day.

337. No handbag limit! (Or hiding them under clothes in the closet)

338. I only have to worry about moving my things when it's time to relocate.

339. I don't have to worry about obligatory check-in phone calls!

340. I can pray out loud without an audience.

341. I'm not ready to start a family.

342. I don't want to get too close to anyone.

343. The only expectations I have to rise to are my own.

344. Committed relationships are boring.

345. I only have to clean up my mess.

346. I am free to explore.

347. I can blast my music without compromise.

348. I simply am not really into people and I don't have to force myself to pretend to be.

349. I am an adventure seeking risk taker.

350. New research shows that lifelong single people are less lonely in old age.

351. Closet space!

352. I can be weird if I want to. I can leave my worries behind...

353. I love to be alone.

CHAPTER 2

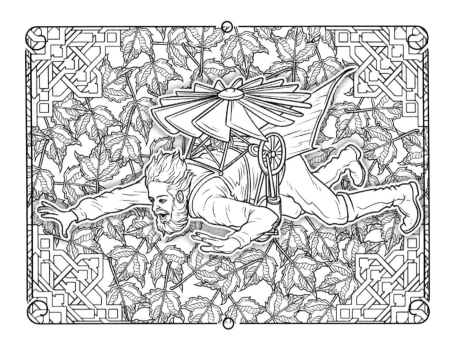

I Think I Can,
I Think I Can

S pread your wings and do all the silly stuff you want! No one is in your way! You can finally get to that ultimate bucket list! There are more things to do each day than there is time on this glorious earth. (Someone still needs to invent a time machine. Is it you?) Just a few of the reasons below ensure that you will not have time for another person! This chapter includes a small sample from the plethora of amazing things you have inside you, just waiting to be recognized. Ready? Get busy with that calendar! Time-is-atickin'!

354. I can swim in every ocean: the Pacific, Atlantic, Indian, Arctic, and Southern.

355. With nobody else occupying floor space, I can move at hyper speed to get a bunch of sh*t done.

356. I can use the extra time for side hustle income.

357. I can now live the van life.

358. I can play solo Cats Cradle.

359. I can be a nomad.

360. I can choose to live or work anywhere. The world is my oyster – I just have to put my finger on the map.

361. I can drift into a beautiful fantasy whenever I want, for however long I want, thinking about whomever I want. It's the sweet life.

362. I can climb a tree (and consider my tree-house plans.)

363. I can take time to get filler or plastic surgery.

364. I can hibernate alone for a really long time.

365. I can leave the dishes out for however long I want.

366. I can change careers whenever the mood strikes.

367. I can go on awesome bike rides with zero destination in mind.

368. I can take a floral, art or sculpture class with the extra time I have.

369. I can make a time machine. (Yeah, I wasn't joking earlier. Get on that.)

370. I can have a backyard movie night and win the coin flip to decide the feature film every time.

371. I can have a living room picnic.

372. I can walk around naked.

373. I can light paper lanterns at the water's edge.

374. I can plan to climb Mount Kilimanjaro.

375. I can learn computer programming.

376. I can lick my potato chips instead of eating them.

377. I can get nostalgic and take a Bob Ross class.

378. I can spend all day in the garage tinkering.

379. I can make a "found footage" movie with my phone.

380. I can marry myself.

381. I can plant a tree.

382. I can take scrumptious naps and spread out like a star fish on whatever surface I choose.

383. I can move to a small island and become the local fortune-teller.

384. I can turn my patio into a beach.

385. I can create a stop-motion video.

386. I can be a total pig when I eat.

387. I can take all my magazines and turn my whole house into a vision board.

388. I can enjoy my passion for silence without distractions.

389. I can be the adventurous friend with juicy life details.

390. I can create an online game.

391. I can get my pilot's license.

392. I can create a board game.

393. I can create a digital game.

394. I can host a bbq with giant outdoor chess.

395. I can make artisan pizza.

396. I can learn how to "remote view" so that I can become a secret spy.

397. I can learn to juggle.

398. I can learn to walk on stilts.

399. I can visit the Pyramids of Giza.

400. Silent time is anytime I'm craving quiet.

401. I can focus on the present.

402. I can make paper airplanes, leave them wherever they land and then call it art.

403. I can invite people over to watch me fly the paper airplanes and call it performance art.

404. I can put crystals all over the house.

405. I can learn origami because those paper airplanes from 402 were weak.

406. I can get lost on purpose.

407. I can learn to play guitar.

408. I can have a big dramatic cry without an audience.

409. I can become a great cook.

410. I can go on a Safari.

411. I can go spelunking.

412. I can write tiny love letters to myself and stuff them all over the house to find later.

413. I can learn kickboxing.

414. I can make a travel journal about traveling alone in unusual places like the Tree House Hotel or the Underwater Sea Room.

415. I can go into an automatic writing state of mind and let myself write an entire book.

416. I can follow my heart in the moment.

417. I can help a neighbor in need by walking their dog or helping get them groceries.

418. I can redecorate the living room.

419. I can make donuts from scratch.

420. I can upcycle things and turn it into a business.

421. I can pace around the house and daydream.

422. I can make trippy stop motion videos about alternate mind states.

423. I can hike Machu Picchu.

424. I can explore the world with google maps.

425. I can make friends with whomever I want.

426. I can learn to knit or crochet.

427. I can take a trip just to gaze at the stars.

428. I can listen to the same song over and over again.

429. I can make a beautiful card for someone.

430. I can enter a marathon.

431. I can make s'mores.

432. I can learn to sink a hole in one.

433. I can make a DIY cornhole game.

434. I can work out really hard and then order a luxury massage.

435. I can spend more time perfecting my social media presence.

436. I can go on an "Eat, Pray, Love" vacation or quest.

437. I can try new food every week.

438. I can have a taco night.

439. I can visualize my desires and dreams through my own POV 'till it comes true.

440. I can jump on a trampoline.

441. I can bake a cake and eat it.

442. I can go to the amusement park with headphones in and ride in the front car of each ride.

443. I can dance like nobody's watching.

444. I can dance like EVERYONE's watching.

445. I can go on a solo photography trip (and NOT share the pictures).

446. I can wake up early just to watch the sunrise.

447. I can install a dancing pole in the living room.

448. I can learn ribbon dancing.

449. I can sleep inside an igloo and spread out like a starfish.

450. I can go dogsledding (with the assistance of far fewer dogs).

451. I can play hide and seek with my dog.

452. I can take myself to a really nice dinner or order-in from a really nice restaurant.

453. I can open a restaurant.

454. I can make a terrarium.

455. I can open a food truck business.

456. I can finally go whale watching.

457. I can knit a scarf.

458. I can learn needlepoint.

459. I can go on a long fishing trip.

460. I can write a book of poetry.

461. I can have a bridge or poker game night.

462. I can take a snowshoe hike.

463. I can call a friend and have a

proper catch-up.

464. I can visit Monte Carlo to watch the Monaco Grand Prix.

465. I can do a jigsaw or crossword puzzle.

466. I can CREATE a jigsaw or crossword puzzle.

467. I can create a list of life goals and begin to check them off.

468. I can write a business plan or help someone else with theirs.

469. I can make a kite and fly it somewhere special.

470. I can learn to make bread.

471. I can become a life coach.

472. I can repurpose old clothing.

473. I can create a yoga retreat.

474. I can play horseshoes.

475. I can record myself singing or doing strange comedy acts and make something out of it.

476. I can make bizarre concoctions in the kitchen.

477. I can go hug a tree (or a whole forest).

478. I can go ice fishing.

479. I can do some Mad Libs.

480. I can learn to play tennis.

481. I can collect coins.

482. I can 3D print images of myself in a starfish position.

483. I can write a hit song.

484. I can ice skate.

485. I can play darts.

486. I can live in a treehouse.

487. I can go back to school.

488. I can learn to play chimes or the steel drum.

489. I can start a business that lifts the spirits of lonely singles.

490. I can make plans to host a Super Bowl party.

491. I can improve my resume.

492. I can write a song but this time it doesn't have to be good to anyone but me.

493. I can play frisbee with the cat.

494. I can establish more eco-conscious habits.

495. I can share something I know a lot about – maybe it'll help some people.

496. I can get a pottery wheel and make epic vases.

497. I can take a flower arrangement class to put in my vases from 496.

498. I'm naturally good with flowers so I can take an advanced wreath making workshop.

499. I can to to the mall and master indoor sky-diving. (Why do people make it look so hard? It's just air blasting upwards... right?)

500. I can learn to draw and use myself as the model.

501. I can have a yard sale.

502. I can bake a pie.

503. I can make sidewalk chalk art.

504. I can join a band.

505. I can have Mahjong pool parties.

506. I can focus on wealth building strictly for the purpose of funding a foundation.

507. I can create an awesome playlist.

508. I can become a DJ.

509. I can make my own jam.

510. I can date whomever I want.

511. I can become a business mentor.

512. I can learn a new language with an online instructor from some far off place.

513. I can learn basket weaving.

514. I can get better at networking.

515. I can start my own currency like the Ithaca Hours.

516. I can visit the Integratron, Mystery Spot, Grand Canyon, Sedona Vortex, Arkansas Hot Springs, Route 66, Waikiki or some other US local treasure.

517. I can get an extra job.

518. I can go on a fast.

519. I can learn to toss pizza dough.

520. I can become an event planner.

521. I can cut out bad habits that are harder to shake when I'm with someone.

522. I can develop an air of mystery and be the one

everyone talks about at the supermarket.

523. I can go live on an organic farm in exchange for room and board.

524. I can start a blog.

525. I can watch every Oscar Winning Film.

526. I can join a bowling club.

527. I can go on a digital diet.

528. I can live off-grid.

529. I can go bird watching.

530. I can keep in better touch with my relatives.

531. I can sit by a stream with a picnic basket and read a novel.

532. I can write a three-part screenplay.

533. I can pluck nose or chin hairs without it being gross.

534. I can join a local meetup group.

535. I can visit Reykjavik.

536. I can try to read every book in the library.

537. I can try to read every book in the bookstore.

538. I can start a local bookstore.

539. I can read for kids.

540. I can start a consignment shop.

541. I can become a nun.

542. I can become a priest.

543. I can visit an Ice Hotel.

544. I can make my own craft beer.

545. I can learn how to make candles.

546. I can learn how to make soap.

547. I can go for regular jogs or walks.

548. I can become great a poker, billiards, bridge or bowling.

549. I can learn to tightrope.

550. I can build a bowling lane for the yard.

551. I can begin to see a great therapist.

552. I can go to more art receptions and museum exhibits.

553. I can create a social media account for my pet.

554. I can study astrology.

555. I can learn tarot.

556. I can learn to surf.

557. I can take a Laughter Yoga class.

558. I can become great at jump rope.

559. I can go to fashion or design school.

560. I can learn Feng Shui and rearrange my space to uplift my environment.

561. I can learn sign language.

562. I can practice the law of attraction by creating vision boards, and saying affirmations out loud.

563. I can start a podcast.

564. I can stay at a silent retreat.

565. I can become a Reiki healer.

566. I can buy a house in another country.

567. I can try to build a time machine. I've done some thinking since item number 369 – I'm not so sure it can be done, but I'll definitely try.

568. I can live in a tiny house and just lay around all day.

569. I can experiment with sound using a string telephone or sea shells.

570. I can live in a cottage in the forest.

571. I can make my own instrument that hasn't been invented yet.

572. I can practice The Five Agreements.

573. I can buy a farm.

574. I can open a cafe.

575. I can hire a stylist and remake myself.

576. I can pat myself on the back and say, "You're doing really well."

577. I can go zip lining in South America.

578. I can go horseback riding.

579. I can figure out my five-year or ten-year plan.

580. I can create temporary artwork, such as an ice sculpture or sand art, and make an event out of it.

581. I can learn the ancient art of fabric weaving, textile creation or try to create Dhaka muslin.

582. I can play chess in the park.

583. I can go play basketball.

584. I can do performance art.

585. I can go to the science museum.

586. I can go to the aquarium.

587. I can have a sleepover and tell ghost stories.

588. I can build my emergency fund.

589. I can have a scavenger hunt.

590. I can grow an herb garden.

591. I can make tea using herbs from said herb garden in 590.

592. I can read The Untethered Soul.

593. I can learn how to sew or design clothes.

594. I can learn how to trade in the stock market.

595. I can find a pair of Jax just like the one's I used to play and get really good at them.

596. I can begin to save for retirement.

597. I can create a family heirloom collection.

598. I can study Sumerian history.

599. I can learn more about my heritage.

600. I can forgive everyone with Ho'oponopono.

601. I can become a (multi) millionaire.

602. I can completely remake myself.

603. I can create a mysterious writing system that future scholars will struggle to decipher.

604. I can go to a nearby place that I've overlooked.

605. I can make an advanced puzzle that is also beautiful woodwork.

606. I can start an Etsy shop.

607. I can play Bingo at the local hall and get really good at it.

608. I can start a clothing resale business (all the space definitely helps).

609. I can learn a higher level of math.

610. I can start a food brand with my best recipes.

611. I can create a dog food delivery business.

612. I can do the What Color Is Your Parachute workbook.

613. I can be perfectly impractical.

614. I can start acting in local theater.

615. I can write a play for local theater.

616. I can have a five minute dance therapy session, and when it's over, I can have another one if I want.

617. I can pursue my desire to be be less hasty and begin immediately.

618. I can renovate a house and get into the house flipping business, or just renovate one for myself.

619. I can volunteer where I know my skills will be helpful.

620. I can make friends with a person older than myself. They might need a friend to talk to, or someone to run errands.

621. I can create a beautiful landscape outside my home.

622. I can try to experience infinity.

623. I can give myself a break.

CHAPTER 3

Just Say No

Tough relationships take work and can cause pain and frustration. Below are just a few reminders as to why the "nuclear family" grass is not always greener. Perhaps you've had some of these experiences or are relieved that there is:

624. No more sitting in the car because I don't want to go inside and deal with them.

625. No one who is always in a bad mood.

626. No one in it just for the money or status.

627. No overly emotional marathons about this or that.

628. No one to put me down.

629. No one to snoop through my stuff.

630. No constant gossip to listen to.

631. No one lying about their feelings (unless I choose to do so myself).

632. No one hogging the TV remote.

633. No arguing over which movie to watch.

634. No one to not see me for who I am.

635. No one I have to pretend to be okay for.

636. No one to fight with.

637. No one ogling other people in front of me.

638. No pressure to take it to the next level.

639. No one to spoil my mood.

640. No one who doesn't keep their word.

641. No pressure to create a perfect night out.

642. No one who makes me feel like I'm being juggled, judged or breadcrumbed.

643. No in-laws to judge me or be awkward around.

644. No one getting mad at me for no apparent reason.

645. No more having to hide receipts.

646. No more having to pretend I like to kiss.

647. No one trying to slow me down.

648. No one to accuse me of cheating.

649. No one clinging and nagging.

650. No one still talking to their ex.

651. No one comparing me to their mother.

652. No one comparing me to their father.

653. No one yelling at the television during sports or news.

654. No one to bother me during the game.

655. No one treating me like a child.

656. No one to not let go when I say, "we're done."

657. No one to ghost me when I thought it was going splendid.

658. No one to give their opinion about what I wear.

659. No one that I have to hide my emotions from.

660. No one to judge me if I'm a bit out of shape.

661. No one who is great at everything except for the bedroom.

662. No one who neglects me when I need to be held.

663. No one who takes too long to get ready.

664. No one rushing me when I'm trying to get dressed.

665. No one who doesn't take out the trash.

666. No toxic person who drains me of my energy, and makes me feel second best.

667. No one who can't get along with my parents or siblings.

668. No one to disrespect the things I care about.

669. No one to feel too old around.

670. No one to feel too young for.

671. No one to tempt me with foods that are bad for me.

672. No loud activities in the other room.

673. No sticky stuff on door handles.

674. No one who only wants me for sex.

675. No one to take my love for granted.

676. No one who is extra possessive, treating me like property.

677. No one annoyingly completing my sentences.

678. No one who doesn't understand my needs.

679. No one who disrespects me (especially in public).

680. No one whom I have to pull it together for on my tough days.

681. No one who makes me feel as though I'm not pretty or handsome enough.

682. No one who makes me feel as though I'm not sexy enough.

683. No one to reinforce my feelings of worthlessness. I'm still cultivating my self-love.

684. No one that I feel I am neglecting.

685. No constant barrage of someone else's ideas on how I should run my life.

686. No selfish person whose life always seems to be more important than mine.

687. No one that I have to feel uncomfortable around when I'm in a low emotional state.

688. No one to make me feel their career is better than mine (even if it's true).

689. No one to keep reminding me about my lack of maturity.

690. No chance someone will have me "under their thumb".

691. No one to compare me to their ex.

692. No one to belittle me while I am feeling uncertain.

693. No unrequited love.

694. No power games.

695. No one who makes a new friend that seems to be something more.

696. No one to challenge the way I enjoy my downtime.

697. No one who turns out exactly like my ex.

698. No one telling me obvious lies to my face.

699. No one lying and me not realizing until it's too late.

700. No one who can't understand it when I need space.

701. No one disloyal in my immediate surroundings.

702. No one to secretly sabotage my efforts.

703. No one with broken ears who continues to say, "What? What? What?" when I speak.

704. No chance I settled.

705. No one zoning out when I'm talking to them.

706. No one to "let themselves go" after I've committed to them.

707. No one walking me into bad situations because I trusted them.

708. No accidental narcissist to trap and confuse me.

709. No accidental pregnancy.

710. No one to tell me my new found spirituality is really a cult.

711. No one to give me anxiety because I love them so much.

712. No one to kill my fresh ideas with doubt and logic.

713. No one to comment on my late night food binges.

714. No one to judge my hole-y (blanket, tshirt, sweats, fill in the blank).

715. No one to accuse me of this or that.

716. No one to reveal seriously weird habits five years into a relationship.

717. No expensive wedding to pay for.

718. No one flirting with my best friend.

719. No having to pretend I'm happy when I'm truly miserable in a crappy relationship.

720. I don't have to say, "no".

CHAPTER 4

Don't Tell Me
What To Do

O kay, so we've gone through the reasons why one may be relieved to have some time alone, but perhaps you also have a bit of a rebel inside – needing to tell the world what you will and will not stand for. It's really nobody's business that:

721. I just don't feel like it. Whatever "it" is.

722. I don't want to lose my independence.

723. I don't need the validation of others.

724. I am living my truth.

725. I don't want to be the one that loves the other more.

726. I don't have to worry about jealous outbursts or draining mind games.

727. I don't have to worry about being breadcrumbed.

728. I don't really want anyone's attention.

729. Marriage is a fragile fantasy if not approached right, and I am not right.

730. I don't have to worry about them leaving me when I get too old.

731. Ageism for unmarried folks of a certain age is so yesteryear.

732. My family is trying to force me into an arranged marriage but I am a pioneer.

733. I don't have to change the way I behave because someone gets insecure too easily.

734. I don't have to clear my browser history.

735. I don't have to share the attention.

736. I am too unique for a relationship.

737. I rebel from the relationship standard of which I am judged and accept that being single makes me happy.

738. I work off my love handles when, how and IF I want to.

739. I am not a hermit, I'm a maverick.

740. I don't want to feel my issues are too much for someone.

741. I don't want to have to worry about taking the sheets. I'm a fitful sleeper who also really does like the starfish position. Double whammy.

742. I don't want to help others with their laundry or clean up a trail of clothes.

743. I don't want to feel obligated to check in. I like to use my downtime to space out.

744. I don't want a ball and chain.

745. I don't care how much pressure is put on me, I am happy being single.

746. I don't want to be broken up with out of the blue.

747. I don't have to worry about them cheating on me with someone at work.

748. I don't have to worry about feeling like my presence bothers the person I'm with.

749. I don't have to say hello to anyone when I get home.

750. I don't have to help process someone else's grief.

751. I don't have to be vulnerable (phew!).

752. I don't want to be a rebound or deal with people's baggage.

753. I am not obligated to attend anyone's work events.

754. I'll take the garbage out without being reminded.

755. I don't want to be the fix-it handy-person of the universe.

756. I don't want to waste years on someone who wasn't right.

757. I don't want to open myself up to a meaningless broken heart.

758. Only the movies make single people look miserable and I'm not falling in line for anybody.

759. I don't have to shower to make others happy.

760. I don't have to wear noise cancelling earphones when I walk through the house because I'm with someone who nags or smothers me with small talk.

761. I don't have to remember birthdays or anniversaries.

762. No pressure to have kids.

763. I choose what I want to passionately devote my time to.

764. I don't have to worry about hidden agendas.

765. I don't want to be the person someone settles for.

766. I don't have to focus on someone else's kids.

767. I don't want to be dragged into pointless conversations.

768. I don't want to MAKE polite conversation.

769. I enjoy when there is less ego clashing.

770. My holiday plans are my own.

771. I don't have someone hollering at me from the other room.

772. I can get married later (if I choose that route).

773. I don't want to open myself up to a "situationship" that's I don't realize is going going nowhere until it's too late and my heart is broken into a million pieces.

774. I don't have to explain myself.

775. I have not met the right match and refuse to be in the wrong relationship because of societal pressure.

776. I don't know what love is yet.

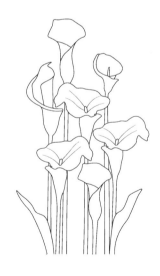

777. For women, marital expectations harken back to institutions built around female obeisance and I am here to challenge the status quo!

778. I will continue to feel wholly enriched and satisfied despite the antiquated and harmful stereotypes given to me by conventional thinking, which have been coined, "Singlism".

779. I am an introvert. We make up a whopping 40% of the population – I'm not strange for enjoying my own company (despite the judgment and my needs being overlooked).

780. I cherish and appreciate my interactions with others more.

781. I really don't care about my bad Single-dom Public Relations.

782. I was obviously born to be wild.

CHAPTER 5

Just in the Nick of Time

○————————————————————○

Time may very well be the most precious commodity of all. We miss it when it's gone and never see it flying away. Think of it like this: if you live to be 80 years old, that means you will have experienced a mere 80 summers, the same number one would find in a small pack of jelly beans! When others aren't constantly in my space, requiring my attention:

783. I have the time to work through why I don't want to be vulnerable, and that could take years.

784. My schedule is my own.

785. I set the alarm clock exactly when I want it to go off.

786. I have the time and space to think through the future I truly want for myself.

787. Time alone is restorative.

788. I have time to figure out scientific mysteries, like dark matter or why gravity works.

789. I have time for all the audio books I have on my list.

790. I can go for a long drive.

791. More time and more freedom.

792. It's easier to live in the moment.

793. I can spend more time at work.

794. I can stare at myself in the mirror until I'm done admiring my beautiful self.

795. I can lay by the fireplace lost in thought while the flames dance in endless shapes.

796. I have the time to start that blog I always meant to write.

797. I can write new code and program a cute robot.

798. There is time to take an art class or learn a new skill, like calligraphy, metal-smithing or dance.

799. Last minute plans are easier.

800. I can have a family when and if I'm ready for one – lots of people are having families later in life.

801. I am part of a generation who can freeze their eggs.

802. I have more time for my pet.

803. There's more time to read.

804. I have more time to concentrate on cooking delicious and healthy meals based on my personal dietary needs.

805. I don't have to worry about someone else's schedule when I want to exercise.

806. More time to concentrate on my finances.

807. I can take long walks and let myself slip into countless daydreams.

808. I can have more guiltless "me" time.

809. I have more time to align my chakras every morning.

810. There's plenty of time to call friends.

811. I can wander through my favorite store for as long as I want.

812. I can make the farmers market a habit.

813. I can go to bed when I want to go to bed.

814. Long showers – just saying.

815. Long baths – let the candles burn low.

816. I treat myself as I would the best lover. Let's face it, I deserve it.

817. Time alone allows me to witness and appreciate the ebb and flow of a story grander than myself, rather than be unsettled by it.

818. I can spend the day in quiet contemplation.

819. Uninterrupted time for my Stockmarket plays.

820. There's plenty of time to figure out my big plans.

821. I have the time to work through mental conflict.

822. I have more time to work on positive thinking.

823. There's more time to... be!

824. I can prioritize things that have been on the shelf for years.

825. There's finally enough time to finish my masterpiece.

826. I can spend time with friends without having someone telling me when it's time to go home.

827. I can shave on my schedule.

828. I can wax on my schedule.

829. I have time to volunteer.

830. I can embrace my own flow instead of incorporating someone else's.

831. I can take the time to grow a garden.

832. I don't have to spend as much time on forced texting.

833. I spend less time on forced phone calls.

834. I have an abundance of time to explore my sexuality.

835. I find myself in healthy contemplation more often.

CHAPTER 6

Getting better all the time

When Siddhartha (a.k.a. the Buddha) sat under a tree to understand the meaning behind suffering, he determined that to remove oneself into a place of solitude was the best way for humanity to evolve. That's just a fancy way of saying, that there are benefits to pain and loneliness. Often, our greatest challenges bring about the most growth and strength. You don't need Buddha's enlightenment to reap the rewards of the rich inner life, healing and self-actualization that living solo can bring. I find that so many things become better when I focus on myself:

836. I am getting better at letting go of the things that don't serve me.

837. I have a rich life full of wonderful friends because Single-dom doesn't mean I don't have relationships.

838. I can get lost in sound therapy with things like a metal therapy drum, sound bowl or chimes and even create my own sound bath.

839. I learn how to uplift myself. It is immeasurably empowering.

840. I can reflect on my feelings and thoughts about religion.

841. I can spend more time healing my critical inner voice.

842. Time alone helps to heal childhood wounds.

843. Societal standards often steer me the wrong way or distract me from my true path.

844. Solo status just feels simpler.

845. Despite my Single-dom, I am a warm person that people can turn to in their time of need.

846. I'm inspired by historical singles like Leonardo Da Vinci, Sir Isaac Newton, Florence Nightingale, Jane Austen, Mother Teresa, Ludwig Van Beethoven, Nikola Tesla, Joan Of Arc, Emily Bronte, Simone De Beauvoir and Octavia E. Butler.

847. My third eye is stronger and I can hear my intuition more easily.

848. When I feel off balance, it's easier for me to realign because I have gained the tools to self-soothe.

849. Autonomy, personal space and freedom are becoming my strong point.

850. I tend not to repeat the same mistakes when I pay more attention to my patterns.

851. I have time to let my mind wander to far off places and bring these visions to life in my world.

852. Every day I am better at observing and shifting my mood.

853. I get better at self-love.

854. The more I truly heal and the quieter it becomes on the inside.

855. When I'm alone, I'm able to see and reprogram deeply ingrained, harmful habits.

856. I am better at appreciating the little things, moment by moment: boredom is a state of mind.

857. Self-reflection empowers my self-confidence.

858. I find I have more time for regular acts of compassion.

859. I can practice focusing on the here and now – a relationship muscle I'm building for a future soulmate.

860. Every day I spend in solitude the more authenticity I am able to build.

861. When I go inwards it allows me to live in the present and it's in these moments of presence I find time slows down.

862. I can clean out all the clutter and get extremely organized so that my life feels lighter and more focused.

863. My powers of observation are heightened when I am by myself.

864. I have the time to create an amazing gratitude list which I can say out loud every day.

865. When I meditate, it's easier to focus on me.

866. I am more in control of mindless consumption.

867. I can go deep within and forgive everyone I need to so I no longer hold the weight of heavy grudges.

868. I can make more time for acts of kindness.

869. Time alone is enriching.

870. Single-dom forces me to face my fears, like meeting new people or going to a concert alone. This practice makes me stronger.

871. Time alone creates space for me to ponder existence.

872. I can figure out my mantra.

873. Solitude encourages more flexibility and experimentation in my life, initiating more self-actualization.

874. Spending time alone helps me honor my boundaries.

875. I get better at identifying the draining individuals in my life and staying clear of them.

876. The more time I spend alone the more conscious I am of using technology mindfully.

877. I am getting better at surrounding myself with people who uplift me.

878. My people skills are getting better and better.

879. I can adopt and create a super family!

880. Solitude can be an empowering and transformative experience.

881. If I am in turmoil, I know it's self generated.

882. I can get to know myself better.

883. I can always ask for help when I need it.

884. I am able to quit my addictions.

885. I am my own judge.

886. I can focus on strengthening my heart chakra and learning to love unconditionally.

887. My confidence is stronger because I have a better relationship with my own self-doubt.

888. I am learning that self-care is not optional.

889. I get better at self-compassion every day.

890. I step outside of my comfort zone and have the privilege of being surprised by my strength.

891. The most valuable relationship I have is with the Divine, the second most valuable is with myself.

892. I have only my dietary restrictions to worry about.

893. I can meditate without interruption.

894. I can do yoga without interruption.

895. When I have more time to myself I am able to tune into the unique quality of my own energy.

896. I can foster a dog and take them for hikes.

897. Time alone allows me to enjoy the little things.

898. It's easier to try new styles without an audience.

899. I go with the flow more easily when I'm alone.

900. My body is my temple and I'm able to treat it as such.

901. I declutter my mind daily.

902. I know when to walk away from situations that don't serve me.

903. Devotion to my autonomy and my path to wellbeing is a trait which I inspire in others.

904. I continually create an environment which allows me to live with minimal stress, and as such, live a healthier life style.

905. I have better command over the mean spirited roommate in my head.

906. My independence becomes priceless and my self worth grows.

907. Solitude helps me to become a better leader.

908. Time alone allows me to honor and understand other people's boundaries more easily.

909. When I am personally fulfilled through self-care, and have realigned with my purpose, I can more easily embody true empathy towards others.

910. I notice when I am doing things that do not serve me, just to please others.

911. I am less hasty.

912. I am less apologetic.

913. I am more self-aware.

914. I am more carefree.

915. I am less apt to mistake other people's bad energy for my own.

916. I am sensitive to other people's pain when I

have handled my own.

917. Spending time alone makes me less afraid of permanent endings.

918. Time alone allows me to reassess my relationship to social media and take a step back if I feel it drains me or leaves me depressed.

919. The more I get to know myself, the easier it is to reimagine a better world.

920. I have good friends that I can turn to in moments of crisis.

921. I secretly hate being single but realize that I'll be a better partner if I can self-actualize on my own.

922. The wet sand between my toes at an empty beach as the sun sets – it's more profound when I'm alone. I believe I've experienced nirvana.

923. I have gotten to know myself and I like me.

924. I can concentrate on my tasks without interruption.

925. I don't need others to guide my life.

926. I might be alone but I'm never lonely.

CHAPTER 7

Extra Credit

○————————————————————○

Extended time alone might be just the thing to help you conjure the inner superhero(ine) you've always wanted to be. It can happen in the most surprising and unimaginable ways. I notice that my life is improving in amazing ways because:

927. I am more humble.

928. I am my own best friend.

929. I have more control.

930. When I'm alone, I can listen to my body's messages more easily.

931. I am learning that the inherent state of my soul is joy.

932. When circumstances are unpleasant, I am able to powerfully self-soothe.

933. I can discover my genius by combining better habits with my extraordinary mental powers.

934. I can brainstorm new things to try. This combined with work ethic is a powerful concoction.

935. I am getting great at habit stacking.

936. Flying solo feels so free!

937. The more I get to know my true self, the more comfortable I am with the world around me.

938. I spend less time comparing myself to others.

939. I am not who others think I should be.

940. Spending time alone is helping me to work out my issues so that when I am ready, I can be a better partner.

941. I have more existential experiences – poetic thoughts with a cup of tea by the picture window while it rains never gets old.

942. I can think more about how to change the world for the better and take action.

943. I can work on my insecurities.

944. I have more time to offer service to those in need.

945. I value my time more and more.

946. It is easier for me to see and act on injustice as I resonate with the quieter among us.

947. Solitude is a great opportunity to practice self-love.

948. I am self-sufficient.

949. Single-dom is a new norm that I am a part of.

950. I am courageous.

951. I allow myself to feel and explore my emotions.

952. I'm learning that it's okay to be selfish sometimes.

953. I can take the love I would give to just one person and give it to everyone, especially my coupled-up friends, because sometimes they're secretly the most lonely – we never know what goes on behind closed doors.

954. I get to witness the world from a different perspective.

955. I feel less overwhelmed because I know I can trust myself.

956. I value quality over quantity.

957. I am truly proud of my achievements.

958. I am less worried about tomorrow, and as such, less stressed in general.

959. I deserve to feel good. If I only feel bad when in the company of others, I choose solitude.

960. I cultivate skills that make me more resilient than partnered up folks.

961. I am proud of my independence, leadership and strength.

962. I set a precedent for what relationships, or Single-dom, should look like.

963. I truly enjoy my "self."

964. The perfect love does exist and it's inside me.

965. I get satisfaction by sharing my heart through small acts of kindness and enriching my local surroundings.

966. My independence correlates with a healthy sense of digital minimalism.

967. I get lost in the zone as I focus on what I truly enjoy.

968. Solitude is the path towards my purpose.

969. I am awakening to my authentic self.

970. I can connect with deeper emotions I have felt too vulnerable to explore in the past.

971. I can actively go after solo pursuits that help me to thrive, discover my purpose and fulfill my passions.

972. I am happy in my own skin and this makes me more attractive to my best match (if I choose that avenue one day).

973. The world praises extroverts but I know there is nothing wrong with me. (Let's hear it for the introverts!)

974. I feel so much more secure when I encounter confusing feelings: whenever I'm in pain, an attitude of gratitude is the cure.

975. I let go of illusions of lack and live fully in the present moment, whether I'm with someone or not.

976. The Universe is made of love – I am never alone.

977. I harness the power of silence to ponder the nature of existence.

978. I have peace and quiet.

979. I am inspired by the vastness inside me and my unrealized potential.

980. To manifest my dreams, I am meeting the Universe halfway and allowing all the goodness to come my way.

981. My discipline is on fire!

982. I am self-motivated and can truly trust in myself that I am reliable.

983. I am finding my voice.

984. I am understanding my boundaries.

985. I surround myself with positive people.

986. Purposeful solitude is a beautiful, empowering and life changing experience.

987. I am living more mindfully every day.

988. When I am in doubt, I've learned that an attitude of gratitude reverses a "lack mindset" every time.

989. Time alone helps me to get crystal clear about what I really want in a relationship.

990. Happiness is something I generate from the inside.

991. As a whole person, I can meet my true match (if I choose that route).

992. My creativity is thriving.

993. I am proud of the way I carefully manage my thoughts as these become my reality.

994. I have observed a lot of amazing synchronicity and am therefore deciding that this is a benevolent universe.

995. I imagine that I have more in common with everyone than not. I send them the same big giant hug that I'd like to receive.

996. There is a grand design that's hard to see from my vantage point – I am open to the idea that I may one day change my mind and fall deeply in love with my one true only.

997. My plans for world domination are getting clearer every day.

998. No matter if I'm in a relationship or not, I make a concerted effort to commit to joy every day.

999. I am a warrior of love committed to sharing unconditionally with the whole planet. In turn, this love comes back to me triple-fold – I am always content.

1000. I complete me.

Which are your favorites?

1001.

1002.

1003.

1004.

1005.

The list doesn't end just because we've reached the end of the book – have any been missed?

1006.

1007.

1008.

1009.

1010.

Subscribe to the Belle Bax newsletter:
https://tinyletter.com/bellebax

Made in the USA
Columbia, SC
21 September 2023